THROUGH THE BAMBOO

THROUGH THE BAMBOO

ANDREA
MAPILI

BYRON
ABALOS

PLAYWRIGHTS
CANADA PRESS
TORONTO

LIBRARY AND ARCHIVES CANADA CATALOGUING IN PUBLICATION
Title: Through the bamboo / Andrea Mapili, Byron Abalos.
Names: Mapili, Andrea, author. | Abalos, Byron, author.
Description: First edition. | A play.
Identifiers: Canadiana (print) 20210215798 | Canadiana (ebook) 20210215933
  | ISBN 9780369102461 (softcover) | ISBN 9780369102478 (PDF)
  | ISBN 9780369102485 (HTML)
Classification: LCC PS8626.A6796 T47 2021 | DDC C812/.6—dc23

Playwrights Canada Press operates on Mississaugas of the Credit, Wendat, Anishinaabe, Métis, and Haudenosaunee land. It always was and always will be Indigenous land.

We acknowledge the financial support of the Canada Council for the Arts, the Ontario Arts Council (OAC), Ontario Creates, and the Government of Canada for our publishing activities.

For Mayari, our moon goddess.
For our ancestors.
For our descendants.
For every Filipinx child.
Our stories connect us.

Through the Bamboo was first produced by Uwi Collective at the Factory Theatre Mainstage as part of the 2019 Toronto Fringe Festival with the following cast and creative team:

Karen Ancheta
Marie Beath Badian
Lana Carillo
Joy Castro
John Echano
Carolyn Fe
Nicco Lorenzo Garcia
Ericka Leobrera
Anthony Perpuse
Angela Rosete

Director and Dramaturge: Nina Lee Aquino
Assistant Director and Movement Director: Andrea Mapili
Set Design: Nina Lee Aquino and Farnoosh Talebpour
Lighting Design: Michelle Ramsay
Composer, Sound Design, and Music Director: Maddie Bautista
Costume Design: Farnoosh Talebpour and the ensemble
Props Master: Farnoosh Talebpour
Producers: Andrea Mapili and Byron Abalos
Associate Producer: Stephanie Jung
Production Manager: David DeGrow
Stage Manager: Victoria Wang
Assistant Stage Manager: Farnoosh Talebpour
Grief Consultant: Andrea Kwan

The play was developed with funds from the Toronto Arts Council's Playwrights Program in 2011 and the Ontario Arts Council's Theatre Creators' Reserve/Recommender Grants for Theatre Creators, with referrals from Carousel Theatre, fu-GEN Theatre, the Toronto Fringe Festival, and Young People's Theatre in 2013; Cahoots Theatre in 2014; and Theatre Direct in 2018. It had public readings hosted by Kapisanan Philippine Centre for Arts and Culture, Carlos Bulosan Theatre, and San Francisco's Bindlestiff Studio. In 2016, *Through the Bamboo* was workshopped with dramaturgy by Paula Wing, and had two public readings at Soulpepper Theatre as part of their Tiger Bamboo Festival. In 2017, the piece was workshopped and showcased again at Soulpepper's Shen Development Series, with dramaturgy by Nina Lee Aquino. In 2018, it was workshopped with Marie Beath Badian and the second-year students from the Theatre Arts Performance Program at Humber College. Nina Lee Aquino dramaturged *Through the Bamboo* from 2017 to 2020.

PLAYWRIGHTS' NOTES

Writing this play was a massive labour of love that took us many years. From the onset, we wanted to write a Filipinx-Canadian story that the kids in our family could see themselves in—something we didn't have growing up. Representation matters so we also wanted it to be big, fantastical, and epic in scale so they could know that their stories and culture are epic as well.

Through the Bamboo was originally inspired by a book Andrea received as a child about the Samal myth of Tuan Putli and Manik Buangsi. This play was inspired by Philippine mythology, but it is not Philippine myth as you would hear in its traditional form. As Filipinx-Canadians we are interested in connecting with our ancestral lands and the richness of our culture, but as settlers who grew up here in Canada, we are also heavily influenced by Western tradition. For *Through the Bamboo*, we were inspired by fantasy and adventure stories like *The Wizard of Oz*, *Alice in Wonderland*, *The NeverEnding Story*, and the Chronicles of Narnia. We created this play through our unique diasporic Filipinx-Canadian lens, and we've reimagined myth and character to reflect those intersections.

Three of our grandparents have passed away and we wish we had the opportunity to speak to them again and learn more about their lives. We hope our play encourages more conversation between grandparents and grandkids and we hope you walk away from this story being curious about your grandparents. If you're lucky to have grandparents that are still alive, we hope you'll be inspired to ask them about their lives—who they are outside of being your "lolo" or "lola" (Tagalog for grandpa and grandma)—we bet they'll have some great stories. And if your grandparents have passed away, we hope this play sparks a memory of them and reminds you that you will always be connected.

A forward slash (/) indicates the point of overlap for the following line.

An em-dash (—) indicates a self-interrupted change of thought or cut-off from the next character.

An ellipsis (. . .) indicates a trail-off or transition of thought.

Text within square brackets ([ ]) indicates an English translation.

GLOSSARY

arnis: a Filipino martial art also known regionally as kali or eskrima

arnis sticks: lightweight and durable weapons made from sticks of rattan

barrio fiesta: a neighbourhood celebration

datu: a title that denotes rulers (variously described in historical accounts as chiefs, sovereign princes, and monarchs)

dayang: a noblewoman

kubing: a traditional Filipino mouth harp

lola: Tagalog for "grandmother"

Maglalatik: a Filipino folk dance that uses coconut shells worn around the body to make percussive sounds

malong: a traditional hand-woven or machine-made multicoloured cloth bearing a variety of geometric or okir designs, and used for a variety of purposes, including as a garment

nanay: Tagalog for "mother"

Pandango Sa Ilaw: a Filipino folk dance where dancers balance candles on their heads and hands

Singkil: a Muslim Filipino folk dance about a princess freeing herself, danced between long bamboo poles that clap together rhythmically

tatay: Tagalog for "father"

Taas Taasan: a fictional organization of rebels in Uwi, charged with helping Nale reunite with Duman upon her return; in Tagalog it means "to rise higher"

Ulop: the name of the island that houses the Ancestral Palace and the waters around it; in Tagalog it means "fog"

Uwi: the name of our fantastical land; in Tagalog it means "to return home"

SONGS AND NURSERY RHYMES

Sa Ugoy ng Duyan

Tagalog
Sana'y di magmaliw ang dati
   kong araw
Nang munti pang bata sa piling
   ni Nanay
Nais kong maulit ang awit ni
   Inang mahal
Awit ng pag-ibig habang ako'y
   nasa duyan

The Swing of the Cradle

English
*I wish that the past was right
   here before me*
*When I was a small child with
   my dearest mother*
*I wish I could listen to my dear
   mother's lullaby*
*Her eternal love song as I lay in
   my cradle*

Bahay Kubo (excerpt)

Tagalog
Bahay kubo, kahit munti
Ang halaman doon ay sari-sari

Singkamas at talong
Sigarilyas at mani
Sitaw, bataw, patani

Nipa Hut

English
Nipa hut, even though it's small
*The plants that grow around it
   are varied*
Turnip and eggplant
Winged bean and peanuts
*String bean, hyacinth bean,
   lima bean*

Pakitong Kitong (adapted from original)

Tagalog	English
Tong, Tong, Tong, Tong	*Tong, Tong, Tong, Tong*
Pakitong-kitong	*Pakitong-kitong*
Kap Kapre sa gubat	*Kap Kapre in the woods*
Malaki at matangkad	*Big and tall*
Mahirap mahuli	*Hard to catch*
Sapagkat siya ay suwitik	*Because they're crafty*

Note: Subsequent verses of this rhyme substitute different vowels. The second verse replaces all vowels with "A," the third verse replaces all vowels with "E," and so on.

CHARACTERS

Philly: Our twelve-year-old Filipina-Canadian heroine.

Mom: Philly's mother.

Lola: Philly's grandmother.

Ipakita: A duwende and Philly's guide.

Giting: A duwende and Philly's protector.

Duwende: Mythological creatures the size of a small child that live in mounds of earth.

Ekek: A messenger and scout for the Sisters from a group of part-bird, part-human creatures also known as ekek.

General T: The leader and mightiest of the tikbalang.

Tikbalang: Mythological creatures with the torso of a human and the head, legs, and strength of a horse; they are the army of the Sisters.

Isa: The current ruler of Uwi and the eldest of the Sisters.

Dalawa: The current ruler of Uwi and the second eldest of the Sisters.

Tatlo: The current ruler of Uwi and the third eldest of the Sisters.

Koyo: Matalino's protector and his number one in the Taas Taasan. Koyo is a siyokoy—an aquatic, green-skinned humanoid creature with scales, webbed limbs, and fins.

Matalino: Matalino the Wise is a seer, the oracle of Uwi, and the leader of the Taas Taasan.

Ancestors: The spirits of the Ancestors. While they never take physical form, they are always there, appearing as light and melody to those who need their wisdom.

Kapre: A giant, tree-like creature that lives in the forest.

CASTING

Filipinx actors are preferred, if unavailable then Asian, if unavailable then persons of colour. The following casting for ten actors is recommended:

Philly
Ipakita
Giting
Lola
Isa / Mom
Dalawa
Tatlo
Matalino
General T / Ekek
Kapre / Koyo

Note: Family friends, duwende, tikbalang, and Ancestors are chorus roles that can be filled by any available actor.

PROLOBUB

The past. LOLA, with her malong, weaves a story.

LOLA: There is a place. A place of islands and crystal blue waters. Where steep, silvery, jagged cliffs plunge into the sea. Where the forest roots are filled with wisdom and branches carry stories to every shore. Where the warm air smells of sweet mangos, and the creatures and humans live in harmony, basking together in the golden light.

ALL: This is the land of Uwi.

MATALINO: Uwi was ruled by the datu and the dayang, who took care of the land and its creatures.

ISA, DALAWA, & TATLO: And together they had four daughters.

LOLA: Every day the dayang would delight all of Uwi by telling stories. Everything was perfect and the land was filled with joy.

Until one day, the dayang fell ill and suddenly died.

MATALINO: Wracked with grief, the datu banned all mention and stories about the dayang.

KAPRE, GENERAL T, IPAKITA, & GITING: With great difficulty, the creatures and his daughters obeyed.

LOLA: Except . . . their youngest daughter, Nale, who could not help but tell stories with every breath. She would share stories about her mother with anyone who would listen, and when no one would, she would speak to the mangos.

GENERAL T: But there was always someone listening.

LOLA: Up in the endless sky, there lived a prince named Duman, who had great powers. Every morning, he woke the sun to paint the land with light.

IPAKITA: Moved by the stories he heard, Duman peered down through the clouds and saw Nale, blissfully picking mangos in the moonlight.

GITING: He appeared to her and knew right at that moment that he loved her and would never leave her side.

LOLA: Duman visited Nale every night and, over many moons, she fell in love with him. They married in a grand ceremony where Duman gifted Nale with a special malong and granted her immortality.

MATALINO: Moved by their love and remembering his own, the datu's broken heart healed. He realized that stories kept his wife's memory alive, and he lifted the ban on stories about the dayang.

ALL: Once again, Uwi was peaceful, prosperous, and happy . . .

LOLA: But the hearts of the Sisters had not healed as the datu's had. Over time, their hearts and minds twisted, and they began to see all storytelling as a betrayal.

ISA, DALAWA, & TATLO: They vowed to gain control of Uwi and ban *all* storytelling.

KAPRE: But to do this, they needed to drive Duman away.

GITING & IPAKITA: They plotted to destroy Nale's marriage.

LOLA: Unbeknownst to the Sisters, Nale's womb had already begun growing with a child.

MATALINO: So when Nale and Duman realized what the Sisters were plotting, they decided they would go live in the sky together. But the journey was very dangerous.

KAPRE, GENERAL T, IPAKITA, & GITING: They mounted a great horse, and as they began their ascent, Duman warned Nale to keep her eyes closed and to never look back.

Snowflakes start to fall.

LOLA: Just when they were about to finish crossing, she heard the gentle voice of her dead mother.

LOLA lovingly folds her malong into the book and places it in a box while the world begins to transform around her.

MATALINO: Forgetting Duman's warning, Nale opened her eyes, looked back . . .

ALL EXCEPT LOLA: . . . and fell off the horse.

SCENE 1

The present. The basement of LOLA's *house, full of boxes filled with knick-knacks, odds and ends, and a lifetime of memories. Family friends and* MOM *are sorting through the boxes.* PHILLY *enters holding a lampshade.*

PHILLY: Don't touch that! Put it back!

MOM: Philly, go back upstairs.

PHILLY: No! They're all crazy! They keep taking all her stuff and putting it in boxes.

The family friends exit.

MOM: Your lola's friends / are just—

PHILLY: Nothing that's supposed to go together is going in the same box.

MOM: Your lola's friends are just trying to help us sort through her things.

PHILLY: I tried to tell them that the green lampshade only went with the tall light 'cause that's the way . . . that's . . . forget it. I'm keeping the lampshade.

MOM: I know you're upset.

PHILLY: I'm fine.

MOM: I'm upset too. Lola's death has been . . . maybe it's better this way. She was sick for a long time. She didn't remember us anymore and—

PHILLY: I don't want to talk about it.

MOM: Now that she's dead, she's at / peace.

PHILLY: I said I don't wanna talk about it. She's gone, I get it.

MOM: Okay. When you're ready, you can come back upstairs.

MOM exits and heads back upstairs.

PHILLY: *(yelling after MOM)* They're even taking the pictures out of the picture frames, you know!

PHILLY starts looking around at all the random things in the basement. She finds a box marked "For Philly" and takes out a kubing.

Weird. I mean . . . thanks, Lola.

PHILLY *pulls a book from the box.*

Through the Bamboo—the book you used to read to me.

The wind breathes through the pages. A malong falls out. She puts the book down, picks up the malong, and puts it on.

Suddenly, PHILLY *hears* LOLA*'s voice singing "Sa Ugoy ng Duyan."*

Huh?

Lola?

PHILLY *looks around, trying to find where the singing is coming from. She looks at the book and goes to it.*

PHILLY *shuts the book and the singing is muffled.*

As the song comes to an end, PHILLY *opens the book and the singing intensifies as* PHILLY *is transported into its pages.*

SCENE 2

A forest. The air is humid and filled with electricity. PHILLY *opens her eyes to find she is surrounded by* IPAKITA *and* GITING.

PHILLY: *(simultaneously)* Ahhhhhhhhhhhhh!!!

IPAKITA & GITING: *(simultaneously)* Ahhhhhhhhhhhhhh!!!

GITING: Nale!

IPAKITA: It's you! It's really you!

PHILLY: Where'd you . . . how'd you do that?

IPAKITA & GITING: Begin the barrio fiesta!

IPAKITA and GITING *dance like light while playing kubings. Hundreds of impish* DUWENDE *flood the forest, scurrying, giggling and leaping.*

DUWENDE: YAY!!!
She's back, she's back now from her fall
Her stories, they will save us all

PHILLY: This isn't happening. I'm not in a forest. I'm just in Lola's basement. I'm going to close my eyes, count to three, and then everything will be back to normal.

The DUWENDE *hush.*

One . . . two . . . three.

PHILLY opens her eyes expectantly. A beat.

DUWENDE: YAY!!!

They begin to chant and dance the Maglalatik.

Isa!
Dalawa!
Tatlo!
Nale!

PHILLY is caught in the middle and tries to escape multiple times to no avail.

PHILLY: What are you—

DUWENDE: YAY!!
She's back, she's back now from her fall
Her stories, they will save us all

PHILLY: Excuse me, I'm lost. Can you help me find my way home?

DUWENDE: YAY!!!
She's back, she's back now from her fall /
Her stories, they will save us all!

PHILLY: Tell me who you are!

IPAKITA: It doesn't matter who we are. It's who you are that's important.

DUWENDE: YAY!!!
She's back, she's back now from her—

PHILLY: Back?

IPAKITA: Uh-huh. We knew you were back because the sky—it's turning gold again! And now we've found you!

GITING: Welcome back to Uwi!

PHILLY: What's Uwi?

GITING: What's Uwi? It *has* been a long time since you've been home.

PHILLY: Tell me who you are.

IPAKITA: I'm Ipakita of the duwende.

PHILLY: Sure. So she's Tita Pita—

IPAKITA: Ipakita—

PHILLY: And your name is?

GITING: My name? My name?! I am Giting, protector of the duwende. The fightiest, mightiest—

PHILLY: Tiniest?

GITING: Who you calling tiny? I'll show you tiny!

> *GITING takes out her arnis sticks and shows off her skills. The DUWENDE oooh and ahhh at her moves. IPAKITA jumps in to stop her.*

IPAKITA: That won't be necessary, Giting. Remember, she's here to end the reign of the Sisters.

DUWENDE: YAY!
She's back, she's back now from her—

GITING: Stop! Get down!

> *GITING grabs PHILLY and pushes her to the ground, hiding her. The DUWENDE all hide. An EKEK flies overhead.*

EKEK: Ekek!

PHILLY: What was that?!

GITING: Quiet!

IPAKITA: An ekek, a courier for the Sisters.

GITING: And their eyes over Uwi.

PHILLY: What?

IPAKITA: Shh . . . if there's an ekek, that means . . .

The ground rumbles.

GITING: Down!

GITING grabs PHILLY and pulls her into a DUWENDE mound, concealing her from sight. A TIKBALANG battalion led by GENERAL T enters.

GENERAL T: Keep your eyes open and sniff for human flesh.

GENERAL T and the TIKBALANG battalion search. Finding nothing, they exit.

GITING: Clear.

PHILLY: What was that?

GITING: Tikbalang. Demon horses.

IPAKITA: And the army of the Sisters. That's the third group of tikbalang and ekek that's passed through since sunrise.

GITING: You're lucky we found you first.

IPAKITA: All of Uwi has been looking for you.

PHILLY: I'm getting out of here!

GITING: Keep your voice down! They'll kill you if they catch you.

PHILLY: Why would anyone want to kill me?

IPAKITA: You're the key.

PHILLY: The key to what?

IPAKITA: Freeing the creatures of Uwi. Freeing your home.

PHILLY: Look, I don't know you and this place isn't my home. Okay, I just gotta find . . . I'm outta here.

PHILLY goes off in search of the way home.

GITING: She's gonna get herself caught.

IPAKITA: *(to DUWENDE)* Everyone, stay hidden. She's our responsibility and we're not gonna let anything happen to her.

GITING: Let's go, we can't mess this up.

They exit after PHILLY.

SCENE 3

The Great Hall of the abandoned and dilapidated Ancestral Palace on Ulop Island. There is a thick mist in the air. The Sisters, ISA, DALAWA, and TATLO, enter wearing malongs.

TATLO: What are we going to do?!

DALAWA: I never thought we'd be back here.

TATLO: We haven't been here since she left.

DALAWA: And you see it too, right? The sky, it's turning gold again.

TATLO: She's back. I thought she was gone forever.

DALAWA: Do you think she's looking for Duman?

TATLO: Of course she's looking for Duman!

ISA: Sisters, control yourselves!

DALAWA: This is proof, the prophecy is real. We're doomed!

ISA: The prophecy is not real. It's a story meant to cause chaos and rebellion and undermine our rule.

DALAWA: Stupid stories.

ISA: We became the rulers of Uwi to protect Uwi. We know what is best. All stories are dangerous because . . .

ISA, DALAWA, & TATLO: Stories lead to betrayal. Betrayal leads to chaos!

ISA: That's right. We have created a perfect world, one free from all stories.

DALAWA & TATLO: Yes!

ISA: We will not let her or those rebels in the Taas Taasan ruin it.

DALAWA & TATLO: Yes!

ISA: We must silence her once and for all.

DALAWA & TATLO: Yes!

ISA: Good. My plan to protect the Ancestral Palace, here on Ulop Island, is underway. What's the status with the search?

TATLO: Our tikbalang and ekek have found nothing. I say we flood the lands and force her to surface! Lift your malongs to the sky and let's use our magic.

DALAWA: But when we use our magic, we get older and . . . closer to death. And also . . . I don't want to lose my beauty.

TATLO: You think I want to lose my strength?

ISA: And if I lose my wits, how will we stop her? We must be strategic with our magic—we cannot squander what little youth we have left. I have a plan. Now that our sister is here, we have a chance to keep our youth forever.

DALAWA & TATLO: How?

ISA: We were here, in this very room, when our sister and Duman married. We watched Duman use his magic to make her immortal. Now that we control his magic, we can use it to transfer her immortality to us. But we must find her first. Command your ekek and tikbalang to keep searching for her in secret. Have them sweep your lands from your palaces to Ulop's shores. When she's found, send word and we'll return here. We'll deal with our dear sister together.

DALAWA: What happens if we don't find her?

SCENE 4

PHILLY, still in the forest, is closely followed by IPAKITA and GITING.

PHILLY: Stop following me!

GITING: *(to IPAKITA)* She can't be wandering around like this. We need her to follow us.

IPAKITA: So . . . did you know that bamboo is in fact a grass and not a tree? Fascinating, don't you think?

PHILLY ignores her and keeps walking.

IPAKITA: *(to GITING)* I guess that didn't work.

GITING: Look, we can help you. Matalino the Wise warned us you might have forgotten your story.

IPAKITA: Aahh! Giting, not so loud.

PHILLY: What story?

IPAKITA: Um, if we could all keep it down with the "s" word.

GITING: See, you don't remember! Matalino is the seer, the oracle of Uwi. He has been in hiding since you disappeared. Come with us.

IPAKITA: Please.

PHILLY ignores them.

It's not working.

GITING: I've had enough of this.

GITING jumps on PHILLY and ties her up.

PHILLY: Get off of me!

IPAKITA: What are you doing? / No no no no no.

PHILLY: Let me go!

IPAKITA: Giting! Think first, act later!

GITING: This is the only way. *You* wanted her to stop and listen. And when she remembers, she'll follow us.

IPAKITA: Please don't be angry at us. You just need to hear this.

PHILLY: No!

IPAKITA: It'll just take a second. This is the—

    IPAKITA looks around to see if anyone is listening.

—*story* you've forgotten.

    GITING pantomimes IPAKITA's story.

Up in the endless sky, there lived a prince named Duman.

PHILLY: Wait, what?

IPAKITA: Every morning, he woke the sun to paint the land with light. One night he peered down through the clouds and saw Nale / blissfully picking mangos in the moonlight.

PHILLY: Blissfully picking mangos in the moonlight. I know this story.

GITING & IPAKITA: Yes!

PHILLY: There's a datu or something, and stories aren't allowed, and she ends up falling off a horse . . .

IPAKITA: She remembers, Giting, she remembers!

GITING cuts the ropes and frees PHILLY.

After you left—

PHILLY: After I . . . you think I'm Nale?

IPAKITA: Uh-huh. And after you left, Duman fell into despair and the Sisters tricked him into giving them his royal malong.

GITING: They tore it into three pieces and used its magical powers to control Uwi and hide Duman.

PHILLY: No, it's just a story.

GITING: Uwi has been suffering ever since.

IPAKITA: But the prophecy says that the day will come when Nale will return to Uwi, reunite with Duman, and end the reign of the Sisters.

PHILLY: My name is Philly not Nale. Listen, I'm twelve. I guarantee you I did *not* marry the prince of the sky. And I'm certainly not here to end the reign of some "evil" sisters—that I don't have!

IPAKITA: You're the one who will save us. Matalino, the leader of the Taas Taasan, has seen it. And he knows everything!

GITING: And as part of the Taas Taasan, we have sworn an oath to fulfill the prophecy upon the return of Nale. We're here to help you.

PHILLY: Wait, you said this Matalino knows everything, right? Do you think he'll know how I can get home?

IPAKITA: Absolutely. He has the wisdom of a thousand—

PHILLY: Then what are we waiting for? Take me to him.

IPAKITA: I will guide you.

GITING: And I will protect you.

PHILLY: Okay. Cool. Which way to Matalino?

IPAKITA licks her finger and puts it in the air.

IPAKITA: This way.

GITING and PHILLY exit, led by IPAKITA.

SCENE 5

ISA is in her palace. EKEK hands ISA a fan and exits. ISA opens a message fan and starts fanning herself. Magically, DALAWA appears as a recording. She is confused and struggling to use her message fan.

DALAWA: How do I . . . oh! Sisters, I don't know what to do. I'm freaking out! Since I've returned to my palace, the creatures have stopped working and I can hear them celebrating. They're even singing. My ekek and tikbalang have captured so many creatures but they're silent when I question them. Should we just hide in Ulop? At least we would all be together. Tell me what to do. I'm scared. Ekek!

The message ends abruptly. ISA *starts fanning herself with two other fans and magically records a reply.*

ISA: Sisters, my tikbalang and ekek have returned with no sign of her. She's not in my land, so she must be in one of yours. I'm sending General T to assume command of your forces. Come to Ulop at once. The wall is almost complete.

Ekek!

ISA *turns and is startled to find* EKEK *directly behind her.*

EKEK: Ekek!

ISA: Ekek! Deliver these messages to my sisters.

ISA *gives the message fan to* EKEK.

Fly fast.

EKEK: Ekek, ekek, ekek.

EKEK *flies away.*

SCENE 6

PHILLY, GITING, and IPAKITA arrive at the shore.

IPAKITA: Here we are at the shore. Giting, it's time for the secret call of the Taas Taasan. Stand back.

GITING takes out a conch shell and holds it to her mouth.

GITING: Sssssssssstttttt!

PHILLY: Seriously?

GITING: Sssssssssstttttt!

Silence.

IPAKITA: I don't hear anything.

GITING: There!

A creature is seen porpoising in the distance.

PHILLY: Is that a . . . mermaid!

KOYO appears in front of them, gesturing with their arms.

GITING: A siyokoy. That's Koyo. They're Matalino's protector and his number one in the Taas Taasan. They're the only one who knows where to find him.

IPAKITA: Koyo, what's wrong?

GITING: Why aren't you saying anything?

KOYO continues gesturing.

IPAKITA: I think they're trying to tell us something.

PHILLY: Oh, like charades. I used to play it with . . . I love this game.

GITING: I got this.

KOYO gestures.

Choking . . . choking . . . you're choking! And there's two sharks. You swallowed a fish bone and you're choking and you can't breathe and it makes you want to vomit.

PHILLY: You lost your voice?

KOYO points to PHILLY and gives a thumbs up. KOYO does more gestures.

GITING: There's a horse prancing . . . and you're dancing . . . it's a fiesta!

PHILLY: There were . . . uh . . . tikbalang! In a boat and . . .

GITING: There's a mouse . . . and there's a dance battle . . .

IPAKITA: Think first, Giting!

GITING: But the mouse is scared so it vomits super far!

PHILLY: What? No! The tikbalang came close to someone . . .

IPAKITA: Matalino!

KOYO points to IPAKITA and gives a thumbs up.

PHILLY: . . . So you distracted them and you got captured.

KOYO points to PHILLY and gives a thumbs up.

IPAKITA: What did they do to you, Koyo?

KOYO gestures.

PHILLY: They took his voice / forever.

GITING: Forever! I got that one.

IPAKITA: Forever?

KOYO nods and continues gesturing.

PHILLY: But you escaped!

GITING: Is Matalino safe?

KOYO nods.

IPAKITA: This is Nale. We need to get her to Matalino.

KOYO bows to PHILLY and then gestures for her to swim out to them. PHILLY swims out and climbs onto their back.

GITING: What about us?

KOYO splashes the water. Two turtles appear.

IPAKITA & GITING: Turtles!

GITING swims out and hops onto a turtle. IPAKITA stays behind.

IPAKITA: *(sings)* Bahay kubo, kahit munti . . .

PHILLY: Ipakita, come on!

KOYO passionately mouths the words to the song.

IPAKITA: . . . Ang halaman doon / ay sari-sari

IPAKITA doesn't move.

PHILLY: What's happening?!

GITING: She sings when she's nervous. And them? They just love to sing.
You can swim, Ipakita! You're not going to sink like a bone.

IPAKITA: A stone. Sink like a stone.

GITING: Whatever! Stop thinking about it and just do it.

IPAKITA: I don't think—

GITING: Act first, think later. Let's go.

> *IPAKITA hops on to the turtle and holds on for dear life as they accelerate through the sea. As they're moving through the sea, KOYO gestures.*

PHILLY: Hey, you two, Koyo is trying to tell us something.

GITING: Redemption.

> *KOYO gestures.*

PHILLY: Boats? Ya, boats. With lots of . . . trees on them! Going towards . . . an island?

IPAKITA: Ulop / Island!

GITING: Ulop Island!

IPAKITA: What would the Sisters need with so many trees?

PHILLY: To build something?

GITING: Yeah, something big.

> *EKEK, carrying a message fan, flies overhead, spots them, and sounds a deafening alarm.*

EKEK: EKEK! EKEK! EKEK!

KOYO, PHILLY, IPAKITA, and GITING stop. KOYO points to the sky. EKEK swoops down and attacks, targeting PHILLY.

GITING: Protect her!

EKEK tries to capture PHILLY and they struggle. EKEK grabs PHILLY's malong with its beak. KOYO, GITING, and IPAKITA try to fend it off.

PHILLY: Let go!

GITING uses her arnis sticks and lands a blow on EKEK, who, dazed, starts to fly away. KOYO throws a spear, grazing EKEK and causing him to drop the message fan into the water. EKEK hurries away.

That was close.

GITING: That ekek is going straight to the Sisters. They're going to know exactly where we are.

IPAKITA: We have to hurry. Koyo, bring her to Matalino as fast as you can.

GITING: We'll go get whatever that ekek dropped. It could be important.

IPAKITA: Then we'll meet you back at the shore.

KOYO does the Taas Taasan sign. IPAKITA and GITING also do the Taas Taasan sign. They head off to retrieve the package while KOYO and PHILLY race towards the mangroves. KOYO drops PHILLY off.

PHILLY: *(shouting to KOYO)* But what do I do now?

SCENE 7

PHILLY is alone in the mangroves. Suddenly, the water rumbles and waves crash and twist. A huge build up of energy. A giant bubble emerges from beneath the water, housing MATALINO, a shrimp.

PHILLY: You're a shrimp?

MATALINO: A tiger shrimp! You're not Nale.

PHILLY: Thank you! My name is Philly.

MATALINO: Come closer.

PHILLY: Ipakita and Giting told me you could help me get home.

MATALINO: That malong . . . where did you get that?

PHILLY: If you could just point me in the direction of a door or portal or something so I can go home—

MATALINO: You look sad. You feel sad.

PHILLY: What? No.

MATALINO: Why are you here?

PHILLY: Can you help me get home or not? Because if you can't . . .

MATALINO summons the ANCESTORS.

MATALINO: Ancestors, I need your help. Give me your wisdom.

The ANCESTORS appear to MATALINO as light and melody. PHILLY cannot see or hear them.

. . . I see.

PHILLY: Uh . . . hello?

The ANCESTORS answer.

MATALINO: . . . But how?

PHILLY: What do you mean?

The ANCESTORS answer.

MATALINO: . . . She's the key?

PHILLY: Are you talking to me?

The ANCESTORS answer.

MATALINO: . . . Granddaughter?

The ANCESTORS answer.

. . . I understand. Maraming salamat.

The ANCESTORS *vanish.*

PHILLY: All right. I'm done. I'm outta here.

MATALINO: I can help you find your lola.

PHILLY: What? My lola is . . . no, you can't help me with that.

MATALINO: A wise person once told me our stories and lives are woven together like the fabric of this malong. So you see, we are always connected.

PHILLY: I don't understand what you're saying.

MATALINO: Your lola is here.

PHILLY: That can't be.

MATALINO: That's why you came here, isn't it?

PHILLY: No, I just heard— I thought . . . I don't know why I'm here.

MATALINO: Tell me a story about her.

PHILLY: Why?

MATALINO: A long time ago I learned that telling stories helps us to remember those that have been lost. She's here. And if you want to find her, you need to remember and let out how you feel.

PHILLY: I don't know how I feel.

MATALINO: Well let's start with remembering how you came here.

PHILLY: I don't know . . . I thought I heard . . . but I never thought . . . I don't know. I was in her basement and . . . I thought I heard her voice, singing—so I opened the book. And now I'm here.

MATALINO: Did your lola sing to you often?

PHILLY: Yeah. Every night when I was a kid. My mom and I used to live with her so . . . yeah. She sang all the time.

> *With PHILLY's memory, the malong glows and springs to life, pulling her.*

Whoa! What's happening?!

MATALINO: You're remembering. The malong connects you to your lola.

PHILLY: She's really here.
So the malong will lead me to her?

MATALINO: Yes. The Ancestors told me you're the only one who can help her. And she is going to need a lot of help.

PHILLY: I'll do anything to help her.

MATALINO: Good. But, Philly, I have seen what will come. The road ahead is filled with unimaginable darkness. Darkness that your lola would never want you to face. You have a choice.

MATALINO summons a bubble.

If you wish, this will take you home right now. Or . . . you can accept this quest: free Uwi.

PHILLY: How can I free Uwi?

MATALINO: Find your lola, reunite her with Duman, end the reign of the Sisters. Then you can bring her home.

PHILLY: But I'm just . . . me.

MATALINO: You're more powerful than you think. You may feel like giving up sometimes, but you can get through anything.

PHILLY: My lola used to say that to me.

The malong pulls PHILLY.

I'll find her. And I'll free Uwi. Then I can bring her home.

MATALINO hands PHILLY the bubble.

MATALINO: The duwende at the shore. They will help you. They won't understand now but they will soon.

PHILLY: Thank you, Matalino.

PHILLY shakes the malong.

Uh . . . it's not working. How do I . . . ?

MATALINO: Remember, if you want to find your lola, you need to let out how you feel. Close your eyes. Think about her. Now, tell me.

PHILLY: The song. It went, umm . . . I can't remember the words, but it went like this.

PHILLY hums, trying to find the tune to "Sa Ugoy ng Duyan," the childhood lullaby that LOLA used to sing. The malong moves, pulling PHILLY.

Whoa!

MATALINO vanishes as PHILLY exits.

MATALINO: May the Ancestors be with you!

SCENE 8

IPAKITA and GITING weave through the forest, led by PHILLY and her malong. PHILLY is humming, still trying to remember the tune of the lullaby.

IPAKITA: The malong is going towards the Cliffs.

GITING: The fan held one of the Sisters' messages, I know it.

IPAKITA: If we could have just opened it, we would have known their plan.

PHILLY: I hope Koyo and Matalino can figure it out. It could help us find my lola.

GITING: *(to IPAKITA)* I don't understand why Matalino would tell her to find her lola. Nale's lola died a long time ago. We weren't even born yet.

Unseen by the trio, KAP, a kapre, follows them, sneaking up on PHILLY, closer and closer.

IPAKITA: Matalino knows what he's doing.

GITING: We need to get her to Duman.

IPAKITA: If Matalino says help her find her lola, that's what we should do.

PHILLY: Come on, let's go.

IPAKITA: Wait a minute, haven't we seen this tree before?

KAP yanks the malong off PHILLY and laughs.

KAP: Yank!

PHILLY: Hey! Give that back.

PHILLY tries to grab the malong but KAP and the entire forest move.

KAP: You take something of mine, I take something of yours.

GITING: It's a kapre.

IPAKITA: A giant trickster that lives in the trees.

GITING: He controls the forest and likes to make people lost.

PHILLY: Give me my lola's malong back!

PHILLY tries again and the forest shifts around them. The trio chase after KAP. KAP sings "Pakitong Kitong."

KAP: Tong, Tong, Tong, Tong
Pakitong-kitong
Kap Kapre sa gubat
Malaki at matangkad
Mahirap mahuli
Sapagkat siya ay suwitik

GITING takes out her arnis sticks and tries to hit KAP, but she can't reach him.

GITING: Give it! That doesn't belong to you.

The forest makes an "A" shape.

KAP: Tang, Tang, Tang, Tang
Pakatang-katang
Kap Kapra sa gabat /
Malaka at matangkad
Maharap mahala
Sapagkat saya ay sawatak

PHILLY: We need that to find my lola!

IPAKITA: How are we going to get it back?

GITING: Go that way! I'll go this way.

PHILLY: Get back here!

The forest makes an "E" shape.

KAP: Teng, Teng, Teng, Teng
Peketeng-keteng /
Kep Kepre se gebet
Meleke et metengked
Meherep mehele
Sepegket seye ey sewetek

PHILLY: Wait. The forest is moving in a pattern! Like that "Apples and Bananas" song.

GITING: What's a apple?

PHILLY: They're just replacing the vowels. They're on "I." Follow me.

The forest makes an "I" shape.

KAP: Ting, Ting, Ting, Ting
Pikiting-ki—

PHILLY: Gotcha!

PHILLY correctly guesses where KAP's going to be and grabs hold of her malong. KAP keeps hold of one end of the malong. They're in a tug-of-war.

PHILLY: This is mine, I need it.

KAP: This is yours, I want it.

PHILLY: Give it back.

KAP: I'll give it back when you give it back.

PHILLY: Give what back?

KAP: Tree!

PHILLY: I don't know what you're talking about.

KAP: You're tricking!

PHILLY: I'm not.

KAP: You're one of those tricking Sisters.

IPAKITA: She's not. This is Nale. She's here to end the reign of the Sisters.

GITING: And she needs *that* to do it.

KAP: You're against the Sisters?

PHILLY: Yes!

KAP: Why should I believe you?

PHILLY: How about this? We'll help you with your tree, and then you give me back my malong.

GITING: No tricking!

KAP: No tricking? Deal.

PHILLY: What's your name?

KAP: Kap.

PHILLY: What happened, Kap?

KAP: See here? This used to be my favourite tree. My best friend. You know what I call it for short? "Tree."

GITING: That's the same / . . .

IPAKITA: Shhhh!

KAP: Isa, the sister, came to me and asked for my help. Someone was cutting down forests in her land and she needed my help to grow trees there. That's totally my thing, so I went and did it. But she tricked me. When I came back, lots of the trees, including Tree, were gone too. But Tree's okay, right?

IPAKITA & GITING: Uh . . .

PHILLY: Once you cut down a tree, it dies. It can't grow taller or give shade or make fruit anymore.

KAP: So Tree's just . . . gone? That sucks. That totally totally sucks!

PHILLY: Yeah, it does. I'm sorry, Kap.

IPAKITA: Yeah, we're sorry too.

PHILLY: You want to tell us a story about your tree?

KAP: Why?

PHILLY: Uh . . . I don't know, maybe it will help?

KAP: I don't wanna talk about it.

PHILLY: I get that.

KAP: But I just . . . I think I need . . . I just
. . . uuuuuuuuuggggggghhhhh!!!

> *In a flurry,* KAP *arranges the trees as the forest moves, creating a garden of flowers in the shape of a "T."*

It's a "T" for "Tree."

PHILLY: Wow. Nice, Kap.

KAP: I just needed to do something, you know? I feel a *bit* better. Still sucks though.

PHILLY: Yeah, I know.

KAP: Here's your malong.

PHILLY tries to grab it, but KAP pulls it away. He offers it again, and she tries to take it, but he pulls it away again. Finally, he gives it to her.

PHILLY: Thanks, Kap.

GITING: I still don't understand why Isa would need so many trees.

KAP: I don't know. I followed the trail of broken branches to the Western Tides and all the trees were on boats with tikbalang. They were talking about a wall or something.

IPAKITA: That's it! The Sisters are building a wall to fortify the Ancestral Palace!

PHILLY: That's why they needed the trees.

IPAKITA: They must be headed back there.

GITING: Why a wall?

PHILLY: Maybe they're trying to protect something.

IPAKITA: Duman! He must be there.

PHILLY: First thing's first. We have to find my lola.

PHILLY starts to hum but her malong pulls her in different directions.

It's acting weird.

KAP chuckles.

IPAKITA: Kap, can you show us the way out of the forest?

KAP points in a direction. The forest shifts.

GITING: Fool me once, shame on you. Fool me twice, shame on . . . you.

IPAKITA facepalms.

Which way is the real way?

KAP points in a different direction. The forest shifts.

PHILLY: Kaaap?! No tricking, right?

KAP points in a different direction.

KAP: No tricking.

PHILLY: Thanks, Kap.

IPAKITA, GITING, and PHILLY head off.

SCENE 9

The Great Hall at the Ancestral Palace on Ulop Island with
ISA *and* TATLO.

TATLO: Where's Dalawa? I should have dragged her here myself.
Are you sure you sent the message saying to meet us here at the
Ancestral Palace?

ISA: I sent it.

EKEK enters.

EKEK: Ekek!

TATLO: Ekek! Where's Dalawa? You insubordinate little—

ISA: What happened? You're bleeding.

EKEK: Ekek, ekek ekek ekek, ekek ekek.

TATLO: A human?

ISA: It's her.

EKEK: Ekek ekek ekek ekek.

TATLO: With two duwende and a siyokoy?

ISA: They found her first. The Taas Taasan. What happened to the message for Dalawa?

EKEK: Ekek ekek.

ISA: You dropped it?!

EKEK: Ekek ekek ekek ekek ekek, ekek ekek.

EKEK is preening.

ISA: Ekek! Don't. Move.

ISA pulls a strand of PHILLY's malong from EKEK's beak.

This is a strand from a malong.

TATLO: Is this from our little sister's malong?

EKEK: Ekek.

ISA: Fly to Dalawa and tell her to come here at once.

TATLO: And if you mess this up again, it will be the end of you.

EKEK flies off.

ISA: With this strand, we'll use our magic to locate the malong and our sister wearing it.

TATLO: But Dalawa's not here.

ISA: We can't wait for her.

TATLO: We swore we would not use our magic unless we all agreed.

ISA: We must strike now or risk her escaping our grasp. Lift your malong.

The two Sisters hold up their malongs. They begin to glow. The glow intensifies. They begin an incantation.

ISA & TATLO: Winds hear us.
Hangin, pakinggan mo kami!

Take this strand and find the malong from whence it came. Carry the voice of the one who wears it to us.

The wind takes the strand and carries it out of the window of the palace.

Meanwhile, PHILLY, IPAKITA, *and* GITING *appear on the Cliffs. The malong is leading* PHILLY *as she hums.*

ISA: I hear something.

PHILLY tires and stops. The malong lies still.

GITING: C'mon, keep humming.

PHILLY: I need to rest a second.

TATLO: It's her. She is talking but I cannot hear who she is talking to.

GITING: If we're going to help you find your lola, we need to know what she looks like. I'll make a sketch of her. Go!

GITING draws on the ground with her arnis sticks.

PHILLY: Um . . . she looks like a grandmother.

GITING: I need specifics! Height?

PHILLY: She's like, this tall.

GITING: Wow, that's huge! Hair?

PHILLY: Usually up in a bun.

ISA: We almost have her.

GITING: Good. Clothing?

PHILLY: Well, at home she likes to wear these duster muumuu things, but when she's out she likes to wear cardigans.

ISA: Closer.

GITING: What colour?

PHILLY: Green mostly.

ISA: Just a little more . . .

GITING: There.

GITING reveals a terrible drawing of LOLA.

IPAKITA & PHILLY: That's terrible.

ISA: Got you! The Cliffs. She is on the Cliffs.

TATLO: Let us end this.

ISA: Winds and rains, hear us.

They hold up their malongs. TATLO begins to chant rhythmically as ISA speaks.

TATLO: Hangin at ulan, makinig sa amin. *[Wind and rain, hear us.]*

The wind starts to blow within the Great Hall and along the Cliffs.

ISA: With the powers of Duman, prince of the sky, we command you, hear us.

The Cliffs. PHILLY, IPAKITA, and GITING are being assaulted by wind and rain.

PHILLY: Where'd this storm come from? Is this normal?

IPAKITA: It is a little peculiar.

GITING: This fast? No, it's not normal at all.

The Great Hall.

ISA & TATLO: Hangin at ulan, pakinggan niyo kami! *[Wind and rain, hear us!]*

Lightning strikes the malongs. Sounds of thunder and screeching winds are heard in the Great Hall and on the Cliffs.

ISA: Mighty typhoon, heed our power! Pound your fists into boulders and crush them into sand. Uproot ancient trees with your howling breath and send their splinters crashing to the ground. Spit, foam, and weep with rage! Drown the earth below your sea.

ISA & TATLO: Open your gates and unleash your fury upon the Cliffs!

The Cliffs. The malong is really pulling PHILLY.

IPAKITA: Let's find some shelter.

PHILLY: The malong says we go this way.

IPAKITA: We'll continue as soon as the storm lets up.

GITING: She's right. It's getting worse. We have to go back!

PHILLY: No, we can get through this.

IPAKITA: If we keep going, this storm will kill us.

PHILLY: She's close. Look at the malong! We have to keep going.

The Great Hall.

ISA & TATLO: Hangin at ulan, makinig kayo! *[Wind and rain, hear us.]*
Thunder and lightning, yield to our command.
Bear our fury upon the land!

> *TATLO throws a lightning bolt and it crashes into the Cliffs, causing the ground to give way beneath* PHILLY, IPAKITA, *and* GITING. PHILLY *holds on but* IPAKITA *and* GITING *fall and hang on to the cliff's edge. They dangle, struggling to hold on.*

PHILLY: Hold on!

> PHILLY *rushes to the* DUWENDE *and grabs their arms.* GITING *loses her grip and begins to fall. She grabs* IPAKITA's *leg.*

Ipakita!

IPAKITA: Hang on!

PHILLY: I can't, you're slipping!

IPAKITA: Giting, swing to the right. You can reach that rock. Giting!

GITING: You have to let go.

PHILLY: What?

GITING: Ipakita, you have to let go.

PHILLY: No! Don't let go!

IPAKITA: If you just swing, you'll reach it.

GITING: We swore to protect her.

PHILLY: No! You can't! I won't let you.

GITING: Our job is to keep her safe. I'm finally thinking first. And now, you need to act.

PHILLY: I command you not to let go. I am Nale. You have to listen to me!

IPAKITA: Keep going, Philly. You'll make it through. Remember your quest: free Uwi and you'll free us all.

IPAKITA lets go of PHILLY. They fall.

PHILLY: No!

PHILLY quickly takes out the homing bubble and throws it at IPAKITA and GITING. The homing bubble envelops them. The bubble protects them and begins to rise. The storm is angered and a tornado erupts. The DUWENDE are caught in the storm. The bubble is violently thrown around and downwards to the ground.

It's supposed to bring you home!

Stop!

Just stop it!

Do you hear me! Stooooop!

The storm stops and the sky clears instantaneously. Shocked, IPAKITA and GITING stare up at PHILLY as the bubble begins to rise, floating calmly. Silence. Suddenly . . .

IPAKITA: I told you! What did I say! She's Nale, princess of the sky.

In the Great Hall the Sisters feel the storm stop. They have aged by using their magic.

ISA: What was that?

TATLO: Something stopped our storm.

The Cliffs.

PHILLY: I stopped the storm?

GITING: We were right. We were right!

IPAKITA: You saved us!

GITING: What is this? How do we get out of this bubble?

PHILLY: I don't know. Matalino said it would bring me home.

GITING and IPAKITA struggle to get out of the bubble. GITING hits it with her arnis sticks.

GITING: We can't get out.

PHILLY: What do I do?

GITING: You stopped the storm. You've remembered. You need to reunite with Duman, and the Sisters' reign will end and we'll all be free.

IPAKITA: Keep going. Remember the secret call of the Taas Taasaan. We'll find you again.

PHILLY: I can't do this without you.

GITING: Find Duman!

The bubble continues to ascend, rising above the clouds and out of sight. PHILLY *is alone on the edge of the cliff.*

PHILLY: What now?

PHILLY *starts humming and the malong pulls her off.*

The Great Hall.

ISA: It just stopped.

TATLO: The air, it is turning away from us.

ISA: What could have stopped it?

TATLO: Do you think it was her?

ISA: No.

TATLO: She does not have powers, does she?

ISA: General T!

GENERAL T enters.

Head to the Cliffs at once. Find her!

SCENE 10

PHILLY, led by her malong, is in a bamboo forest. She tries to keep humming but can't remember the rest of the tune.

PHILLY: I can't remember the rest.

The malong lies still.

Matalino said telling stories would work so . . . right. Lola, Lola, Lola. Well, she's got this big house, but for some reason she only uses one floor.

The malong flutters.

She's got everything there, her clothes, a little kitchen, bathroom. There's a pile of slippers at the door for, like, thirty people. And she's always got fresh fruit, like bananas and oranges and . . .

LOLA: *(off stage)* Mango.

PHILLY: Huh?
She always used to say—

LOLA: Mango?

> *LOLA appears and PHILLY's malong flies off of her and into LOLA's hands.*

PHILLY: Lola?

LOLA: You are not a mango!

PHILLY: Lola!!!

LOLA: Seek, seek. Go, go.

PHILLY: I can't believe it. / You're alive!

> *PHILLY runs and hugs LOLA.*

LOLA: You are not a mango. Who are you? Go!

PHILLY: No, Lola, Lola, / it's me, Philly!

LOLA: Don't come near me!

> *A beat.*

PHILLY: You're still sick.

It's me, Philly, your granddaughter. / It's okay, it's okay, you're just having another episode.

LOLA: Seeking, seeking. High, low.
Mango. Mango.

PHILLY: What are you—what mango?

LOLA points over the cliff, down to the waters below, towards the beach and Western Tides.

LOLA: No going back, no time to roam.
Foggy mist and moonlit home!

LOLA looks at the malong.

PHILLY: That's right, Lola. I'm gonna bring you home. We're gonna go home.

LOLA puts on the malong. Suddenly the malong magically weaves a memory around LOLA—her last memory with Duman, riding a horse to the sky.

LOLA: Duman?

LOLA hears the voice of her mother singing. LOLA looks back towards her mother's voice.

Nanay?

As LOLA falls, the memory begins to fade.

Nanay?
Foggy mist . . . missed . . . missed you—wept and wept
I heard your voice, looked back and leapt.
I remember it all, Nanay—I have no regrets
I'll tell your story, won't let them forget.

LOLA weeps. The sky cries with her.

PHILLY: Lola . . . you're Nale.

GENERAL T and two TIKBALANG surround them.

GENERAL T: Well, well, well. Nale, the traitor. And an extra prize! All alone in this bamboo forest.

PHILLY: Don't come near us!

GENERAL T: Her Majesty Dalawa is on her way to her dock. She'll be happy to see you again. But *you* won't be so happy to see *her*.

PHILLY: Get your hooves off us!

GENERAL T: Silence, prisoner.

The wind intensifies.

LOLA: The wind screams through the bamboo, can you hear it? This place . . . this place, we should not have come near it.

Suddenly, bamboo stems shoot up and bend, falling and wrapping around GENERAL T, PHILLY, LOLA, and the TIKBALANG's ankles. PHILLY screams.

GENERAL T: Argh! The forest, it's alive!

PHILLY: What's happening? My ankles!

LOLA: Princesses break free, so up with your shoe
Don't need a prince. Me first and then you.

> *LOLA quickly steps through the bamboo and PHILLY follows her every step, mimicking the dance of the Singkil through bamboo poles. GENERAL T breaks free and begins to chase them.*

GENERAL T: You can't escape me!

PHILLY: Lola, you made sense! How do you know where to step?

LOLA: Step after step, faster, move through.
Don't look back, go through the bamboo!

GENERAL T: Come back here!

> *The bamboo wraps around PHILLY, enveloping her.*

PHILLY: I can't move. Lola, help me, I'm trapped!

LOLA: Lola? That's me.
And it's you, Philly!

PHILLY: You remember me!

GENERAL T: Gotcha.

*GENERAL T grabs LOLA's arm. The TIKBALANG free them-
selves and head towards them.*

PHILLY: No! Get your hooves off her!

GENERAL T: I have who I came for. The forest will finish you off.

GENERAL T, LOLA, and the TIKBALANG exit.

*PHILLY is trapped in bamboo and struggles to escape.
Kicking and screaming, she thrashes, using all her might,
trying to force her way free. The more she fights, the tighter
the grip becomes—paralyzing her movement.*

PHILLY: Let her go, you . . . you . . .
What . . . what's . . .
Get back here!
What's happening? I can't . . .
Come back!
Let me go!
Don't leave me! Lola . . . wait! Don't leave me! I can't . . . I can't do
this without you. I can't lose you again. Lola! I can't, I can't, I can't,
I CAN'T!

PHILLY surrenders to the struggle. An eternity in a moment.

*The ANCESTORS appear to PHILLY, pulsating as light and
melody, singing "Sa Ugoy Ng Duyan."*

PHILLY: What are you?

A vision of LOLA appears.

Lola.

LOLA joins the ANCESTORS' song.

LOLA: Nais kong maulit ang awit ni Inang mahal

LOLA gestures, passing the song to PHILLY. PHILLY remembers the words and alone sings . . .

PHILLY: Awit ng pag-ibig habang ako'y nasa duyan

I remember the words.

LOLA and the ANCESTORS disappear. The bamboo releases PHILLY.

Thank you, whoever you are.

A beat.

Gotta keep going.

SCENE 11

PHILLY, still deep in the forest. No one is around. She doesn't know which way to go. She checks out different options and trips over a conch shell.

PHILLY: Ow!

A beat. PHILLY remembers something.

I know! Sssssssttt!

IPAKITA & GITING: *(off stage)* Sssssssttt!

PHILLY: Sssssssttt!

IPAKITA & GITING: *(off stage)* Sssssssttt!

IPAKITA and GITING enter.

PHILLY: Ipakita! Giting!

GITING: Philly, we found you!

PHILLY: How'd you find me so fast? You'll never believe what happened—

IPAKITA: The bubble brought us back to our village—

GITING: Koyo's at the shore—

PHILLY: I was trapped in bamboo—I never thought I'd see you again—

GITING: We've been racing back to find you—

PHILLY: I found my lola but then the tikbalang found us—

IPAKITA: All the duwende are in hiding—

PHILLY: But my lola—the way she moved . . .

GITING: The tikbalang burned our village to the ground. / Philly, everything is gone, everything!

PHILLY: They took her and left me but then I remembered her song / and . . .

IPAKITA: They're terrified.

PHILLY: She's Nale!

IPAKITA: What?

PHILLY: My lola is Nale. Nale is my lola.

IPAKITA: But you're Nale. You stopped the storm.

PHILLY: I know I stopped the storm but—

GITING: Get down, hide!

PHILLY, IPAKITA, and GITING hide. DALAWA enters with her entourage. GENERAL T enters with LOLA.

GENERAL T: Your Majesty, Dalawa.

GITING grabs her arnis sticks and starts to go towards GENERAL T.

GITING: Let me at him!

IPAKITA: No, Giting!

IPAKITA holds her back.

DALAWA: What are you doing here in my lands, General T?

LOLA: Dalawa?
Is it true? Talaga? *[Really? Is it true?]*

GENERAL T: Your sisters sent me here. We found her, Your Majesty. I captured her in the bamboo forest.

DALAWA: You!

LOLA: Why am I your prisoner? Has it been so long?
And is that a piece of Duman's malong?

DALAWA: Why are you rhyming like that? You shouldn't have come back here.

LOLA: I came for Nanay, Tatay, you, and me
I came to reunite our family.

DALAWA: You are not welcome here. We are the protectors and rulers of Uwi now.

LOLA: How can you say that? How can that be?
What about Mother, Father, and me?
Don't you remember the songs that Nanay would sing?
And the comfort and joy her stories would bring?

DALAWA: Stop! I will not let you bring chaos back to this perfect land we've created. Memories are stories and *all* stories are forbidden.

LOLA: Stories helped me feel better, it was how I grieved.
I never meant to hurt you. We were all bereaved.

DALAWA: I don't care about the past.

LOLA: But what about us? Remember how we played?
When we would swim in the ocean and put our hair in a braid?

DALAWA: No more stories! When we reach Ulop Island, we'll silence you forever.

LOLA: We are family, Dalawa, and you have a grandniece.
She's trapped in the bamboo and will die 'cause of this beast.

DALAWA: An heir?

GENERAL T: It was just a little girl. I left her tangled in the roots. The forest will finish her off.

DALAWA: Go finish her off yourself and make sure the job is done!

LOLA: No!

DALAWA: *(to another TIKBALANG)* Gag her, bind her, and get her on the boat. Prepare to launch at once!

GENERAL T and the TIKBALANG oblige.

IPAKITA: She *is* Nale.

GITING: They're going to the Ancestral Palace on Ulop Island.

PHILLY: We have to save her.

IPAKITA: And reunite her with Duman.

GITING: But how are we gonna do that if we don't even know where he is?

IPAKITA: First thing's first. We need to get Nale back. But how?

PHILLY: I have an idea. We'll need Koyo and the siyokoy.

PHILLY follows IPAKITA and GITING off.

SCENE 12

*DALAWA's royal flat bamboo boat, on the Western Tides.
DALAWA waits under a canopy in the centre of the boat
while TIKBALANG row. LOLA is bound and gagged. They
row through a thick fog.*

DALAWA: Row faster! Look at my grey hair, sister. Look what you
made them do. But just wait until you see their faces. Isa and Tatlo
are going to be so surprised when I walk in with you.

*The beautiful and haunting voices of the siyokoy are heard.
The TIKBALANG are hypnotized by the sound and stop
rowing.*

You fools! Don't listen to their song! Row faster! We need to get
away from here!

KOYO pulls a TIKBALANG off the boat silently.

I'm warning you! I'll use my magic (even though I'm not supposed to).

KOYO pulls the other TIKBALANG off the boat silently.

Show your faces, siyokoy! I'll fry you fishes!
(Sorry, sisters.) Hangin at ulan, pakinggan n'yo ako.

*A storm begins to form. Unseen by DALAWA, KOYO places
PHILLY on the boat.*

PHILLY: Stop!

DALAWA: Who are you?

PHILLY: Give me my lola back.

DALAWA: You're the heir! Didn't your lola ever teach you to respect your elders, little girl? Bow to me at once. No? You insolent little child. Seize her!

PHILLY: Your tikbalang are gone and you're all alone. Untie her and give her to me!

KOYO places GITING and IPAKITA onto the boat behind DALAWA.

DALAWA: You want your lola? Come and get her.

Hangin at ulan, makinig kayo! *[Wind and rain, listen!]*
Hangin at ulan, makini— *[Wind and rain, liste—]*

Before DALAWA can finish her incantation, IPAKITA and GITING charge at DALAWA.

What? Who are—runts?
Hangin at ulan, makinig kayo! *[Wind and rain, listen!]*

DALAWA throws a cyclone. GITING and IPAKITA are blown off the boat into the water.

PHILLY: Giting, Ipakita!

DALAWA: Do you want to see what I can do to you?

PHILLY goes down to her knees.

PHILLY: You're right, you're right. I bow to you, Your Majesty. You are the rightful ruler of Uwi.

DALAWA: That's more like it.

PHILLY: I just want my lola back. Please . . . let her go and . . . and we'll leave! We'll go back home and Uwi can be yours forever.

DALAWA: See how she begs, sister?

PHILLY shuffles to DALAWA's feet and then . . . PHILLY grabs DALAWA's malong.

PHILLY: Yank!

PHILLY passes the malong to GITING.

DALAWA: My malong! Noooooo!!!

GITING passes the malong to IPAKITA.

IPAKITA: And now that we have your malong, you have no more power.

IPAKITA passes the malong to GITING. DALAWA intercepts the malong but PHILLY grabs it and tears it in two.

DALAWA: No!

GITING: We're taking this boat and you can't stop us.

DALAWA: This is my boat! Mine! I rule Uwi. Get off my boat at once or else I'll . . . I'll . . .

GITING: Koyo, take her over there and leave her on the branches of that mangrove.

KOYO nods and exits with DALAWA. PHILLY frees LOLA.

PHILLY: Lola, are you all right?

LOLA: Oh Philly, my dear.
How'd you get here?

PHILLY: My friends helped me.

IPAKITA: Hello, Your Majesty, Nale.

GITING: Hi. Big fan.

PHILLY: Lola, we need to get you to Duman. The prophecy says that once you reunite with Duman, your sisters' reign will end and the creatures of Uwi will be freed. Do you know where he would be?

LOLA: Waiting for me by our mango tree.

PHILLY: Of course! Where you would tell each other stories. Let's go.

GITING: It's time to send the signal to Matalino.

SCENE 19

On the Eastern Tides, MATALINO waits in his bubble. DUWENDE are in boats and siyokoy are in the water as they wait for the signal to attack the Ancestral Palace on Ulop Island.

MATALINO: Mga Kababayan. *[Fellow countrymen.]*

PHILLY, LOLA, IPAKITA, and GITING are still on DALAWA's boat on the Western Tides. KOYO enters.

GITING: It's time, Koyo.

MATALINO: My friends. Our time has come.

GITING gives IPAKITA one of her arnis sticks.

GITING: Act first, think later.

MATALINO: Nale has returned to fulfill the prophecy.

IPAKITA: Think first, and then act.

GITING and IPAKITA embrace.

MATALINO: The Sisters have silenced our stories for too long.

GITING climbs onto KOYO's back and uses the Taas Taasan conch, signalling MATALINO to begin the attack.

GITING: Sssssssttttt!

MATALINO: Ssssssssttttt!
This is the moment we have waited for.

> *KOYO gestures "good luck" and the Taas Taasan sign. KOYO and GITING race to the Eastern Tides.*

PHILLY: Let's go, Lola.

MATALINO: Duwende tribes, pick up your sticks! Siyokoy, take up your spears! I call on the light of our ancestors to lead us into battle!

> *The ANCESTORS glow.*

IPAKITA: It's time for the Taas Taasan to rise.

MATALINO: Mga Kababayan, it is a new day for Uwi! Charge!

> *They all cheer and charge into battle.*

SCENE 14

ISA and TATLO are in the Great Hall. There's a loud crash.

ISA: We're under attack!

TATLO: Ekek, sound the alarm!

EKEK: *(off stage)* EKEK! EKEK! EKEK!

ISA: General T!

GENERAL T enters.

Where is Dalawa?

GENERAL T: I captured the traitor and handed her over to Her Majesty, Dalawa, at her dock. She should be here by now.

Crash!

TATLO: They want a war—we'll give them a war!

ISA: Raise your malong with me, sister. It's time to show these fools just how powerful we are. General T! Order all tikbalang to the East Wall at once.

GENERAL T exits.

We'll end this with one swift blow.

ISA and TATLO hold their malongs to the sky.

ISA & TATLO: Hangin at tubig, makinig sa amin.
Hangin at tubig, lumamig kayo!
Hangin at tubig, makinig kayo!
Hangin at tubig, lumamig kayo!

> *An eerie silence falls over the Eastern Tides. Then the sound
> of a freezing gust of wind approaches and grows louder.
> The sound of water freezing and the rhythmic pounding of
> TIKBALANG hooves. The Sisters age.*

> *Meanwhile, PHILLY, LOLA, and IPAKITA are on their way to
> the mango trees.*

PHILLY: The diversion worked!

IPAKITA: Why is it so cold? *(sings)* Bahay kubo, / kahit munti . . .
[Nipa hut, even though it's small . . .]

PHILLY: We need to hurry. Lola, which way from here?

LOLA: The garden is around this corner, we're very near.

> *GENERAL T enters.*

GENERAL T: Gotcha again!

PHILLY: Let go of her!

GENERAL T: I thought the forest finished you off.

IPAKITA: Nooooo!

IPAKITA, wielding her arnis stick, rushes and fights with GENERAL T, who holds LOLA in one hand while fighting. IPAKITA is disarmed and captured. PHILLY starts to rush in to help.

LOLA: Stay back, Philly.

PHILLY: But . . .

IPAKITA: You're our only hope. It's over if he catches you too.

LOLA: You know where you need to go! You know what you need to do.

IPAKITA: Find him and then find us!

PHILLY: I'll find you again!

GENERAL T: Get back here!

PHILLY exits. GENERAL T exits with his prisoners.

ISA and TATLO back in the Great Hall.

DALAWA enters, dishevelled.

DALAWA: Uggghh!!!

TATLO: Dalawa.

ISA: What took you so long?!

DALAWA: I was trapped on a tree in the middle of the Western Tides. But then the air turned cold and the water . . . it became hard. I walked here.

ISA: What happened to your malong?

DALAWA: I had to fix it on the way over here. I was ambushed during the crossing.

TATLO: By whom?

DALAWA: A couple of runts—a little girl and . . . her!

GENERAL T enters with LOLA and IPAKITA as prisoners.

GENERAL T: Your Majesties, I present to you: Nale the traitor.

LOLA: My sisters! It's been so long.
I'm not a traitor. Tell him he's wrong.

ISA: Well done, General T.
You should have never come back.

DALAWA: Where is the girl? The granddaughter?

TATLO: Granddaughter?

ISA: There's an heir?!

LOLA: Where Duman is. She's there.

TATLO: Impossible! We have imprisoned him where no one will find him.

ISA: And now that we are all together, we will put an end to you and your immortality will be ours.

> *A TIKBALANG enters with MATALINO, KOYO, and a gagged GITING as prisoners.*

Look what we have here.

TATLO: *(to KOYO)* You again!

ISA: And Matalino "the Wise."

IPAKITA: Giting!

TATLO: Shut your mouth, runt! We're talking to the shrimp.

MATALINO: Nale, my dear. You've come back home! I thought I would never see you again.

LOLA: Your voice is familiar. Are you someone I know?
It reminds me of memories / from so long ago.

ISA: Enough with reunions. Your rebellion has failed.

MATALINO: Isa, Dalawa, Tatlo . . . it's been a long time. I've missed you all.

IPAKITA: Missed?

TATLO: How dare you try to overthrow us.

DALAWA: Uwi was finally at peace.

MATALINO: There was no peace, no freedom. You silenced our stories—

ISA: And now you will watch as we silence your beloved daughter forever!

TATLO: Her immortality will be ours!

ISA: General T!

GENERAL T moves LOLA to the centre of the room.

MATALINO: Stop! Stop!

LOLA: I shouldn't have run away from you three.
I turned back because Nanay's voice called to me.

ISA: Silence! We have forgotten about her. And we will soon forget about you.

MATALINO: This is all my fault. I forbade you talking about your mother because it was what I needed. But Nale *needed* to tell stories about Nanay.

TATLO: The past is in the past! No more stories!

DALAWA: No more betrayal! No more chaos!

MATALINO: Nale's stories were not a betrayal. Everyone grieves differently. But you never allowed yourselves to grieve. Instead, you silenced all stories in Uwi, but Uwi and her creatures are not yours to control.

ISA: Enough! Sisters, lift your malongs. Pour all of your selves into this final moment and we will rid ourselves of loss and pain. We will live forever.

The Sisters gather around LOLA and begin an incantation. A magical bubble surrounds them as Uwi grows darker and a storm grows.

SISTERS: Hangin at ulan, makinig kayo! *[Wind and rain, listen!]* Kailangan namin ang inyong lakas! *[We need your strength!]*

The Sisters continue to repeat their incantation and grow in strength.

LOLA: You never expressed.
You pushed away pain and feeling depressed.
But now we can help each other,
Heal *together* and grieve our mother.
Please, sisters, listen to me.
What's happening now? It feels foggy.

PHILLY enters and tries to get to LOLA, but bumps into the magical bubble and cannot get to her.

Memories are drifting from near to far
And sudden now, jumbled words my are.

PHILLY: Lola!

LOLA: Words my are . . .

PHILLY: I couldn't find him!

LOLA: Memories far . . .

PHILLY: Duman wasn't in the garden!

LOLA: Far . . .
Are . . .
Far . . .

PHILLY: What are they doing to you?

LOLA shrieks in pain as the Sisters' spell intensifies.

Fight it, Lola! I can't lose you again!
Stop! Stop! She's your sister! Don't you remember?

MATALINO: I've lost them and now all is lost.

PHILLY: No, you can't give up! You told me that to find my lola I needed to let out how I feel. You said tell stories. You said remember. And I do. I remember reading your books, and dried flowers falling out when I turned the page. I remember you telling me all the names of your plants. I remember my birthday cards and the special words you'd underline. How we played charades and laughed so hard. How you taught me to shoot a basketball— How you held me when I didn't make the team, the way you brushed my hair out of my face, the smell of your sweaters, the bedtime stories, the way you'd sing to me . . .

LOLA: Singing . . . sing . . . sing.

PHILLY: Singing, yeah, singing! Sing with me.

ISA: Let's end this!

PHILLY: *(sings)* Sana'y di magmaliw ang dati kong araw—

> *LOLA's malong comes alive with golden light and envelops the Sisters as the singing crescendos.*

DALAWA: What's happening?

PHILLY & MATALINO: Nang munti pang bata / sa piling ni nanay—

ISA: Stop singing!

TATLO: Don't listen to them.

ISA: Don't let go.

PHILLY, MATALINO, & LOLA: Nais kong maulit / ang awit ni inang mahal—

DALAWA: I can't hold it!

TATLO: It's too strong!

Awit ng pag-ibig / habang ako'y // nasa duyan—

DALAWA: Oh no!

DALAWA & TATLO: No!

DALAWA, TATLO, & ISA: No!!!

> *The Sisters' malongs abandon them and swirl together. The malong reunites with* LOLA. *Suddenly, the golden light spills out over all of Uwi, restoring the land and its creatures.* MATALINO *transforms back into his human form as datu of Uwi.* KOYO's *voice returns as he sings "ahhhh" to a crescendo.* GENERAL T *is freed from the Sisters' command. The Sisters have aged and are stripped of their powers.*

LOLA: Duman! I'm home and our home has returned to us.

> PHILLY *runs to* LOLA *and embraces her.*

PHILLY: Lola!

LOLA: My precious Philly!

PHILLY: You're better—you're not rhyming anymore!

> LOLA *spots* MATALINO.

LOLA: Tatay!

> LOLA *hugs* MATALINO.

MATALINO: My daughter . . . you're home.

LOLA: Philly, come here. This is your great grandfather, the datu of Uwi.

PHILLY: You're the what?

MATALINO: You did it. You found your lola and you brought her home.

GITING: What are we going to do with them?

LOLA goes to her sisters.

LOLA: You were never able to express your pain and sadness when Nanay died. But I hope you can now. Our stories and lives are woven together like the fabric of this malong. We are always connected.

ISA: She used to say that . . . Nanay.

DALAWA: Nanay.

TATLO: Nanay.

The four sisters hold hands for a moment.

MATALINO: You have done much damage to Uwi and its creatures. I will meet with all of the creatures you have harmed and, together, we will decide what's next for you. It's going to take time to regain their trust. But that will be for another day. Today, we rejoice. For Uwi is free again.

LOLA: Nanay's memory is alive again. And so now I can go.

PHILLY: Yeah, Mom's probably worried sick about us. Come on, Lola, let's go home.

MATALINO: It saddens me to see you leave, but you're right, it's time for you to go home. Thank you for all you've done for Uwi.

PHILLY hugs MATALINO.

KOYO: Thank you for helping us and for saving Uwi, Philly.

PHILLY: Your voice is back!

KOYO does the Taas Taasan sign. PHILLY does it back.

I'm so happy I got to meet you all. I'll miss you, Giting! I'll miss you, Ipakita.

IPAKITA and GITING hug PHILLY.

LOLA: Take this.

LOLA gives PHILLY her malong. MOM's voice calls from home.

MOM: Philly . . . Philly!

PHILLY: Mom?

LOLA: Home is calling you, Philly.

PHILLY: Don't you mean us?

LOLA: Just like my home is calling me.

PHILLY: But . . . aren't you coming with me?

LOLA: I've done what I came to do and now I'm going to the sky. Duman's waiting for me.

PHILLY: But I thought—the prophecy, we saved Uwi—I did all the things. You're supposed to be with me.

A gentle snow begins to fall.

LOLA: I'm going home now and it's time for you to go home too.

PHILLY: But I need you.

LOLA: Whenever you miss me, remember our time together.

PHILLY: No! You can't leave me again. I don't want to leave without you.

LOLA: We will always be connected.

PHILLY: Lola . . . Lola!

LOLA: Goodbye, Philly. I love you.

The wind intensifies.

PHILLY: No! Lola!

Snowflakes continue to fall.

LOLA: Thank you for helping me—for helping all of us.

SCENE 15

PHILLY is back in LOLA's basement. She has LOLA's malong.

PHILLY: Lola! Lola!

MOM enters and wakes PHILLY up.

Mom, I'm sorry. I'm sorry, I couldn't do it. I couldn't bring her back! Ipakita and Giting went home in the bubble and / Matalino was the datu—

MOM: Shh shh shh, it's okay. It's okay.

PHILLY: I'm sorry, I'm sorry! It wasn't enough. I still couldn't . . . I couldn't bring her back.

MOM: It's not your fault.

A beat.

PHILLY: I miss her.

MOM: I miss her too. But she'll always be with us.

PHILLY: 'Cause we're always connected?

MOM wraps the malong around PHILLY.

MOM: We can keep her memory alive when we remember her and tell stories about her.

PHILLY: And it's like she's with us again, right?

MOM: That's right.

PHILLY: Like that time when Lola and me went camping in the backyard and we accidentally burned down the tent?

MOM: Yes, just like that.

A beat.

PHILLY: Can you tell me about how Lola met Lolo?

MOM: Your lola was a great storyteller. When she was young, she was always telling stories. And when no one would listen, she would speak to the mangos. One night, Lolo saw Lola . . . he saw her . . .

A beat. She struggles to continue.

PHILLY: Mom, it's okay. It's okay to be sad. One night, Lolo saw Lola blissfully picking mangos in the moonlight. He knew right at that moment . . .

PHILLY becomes the storyteller and passes the story on.

. . . that he loved her and would never leave her side. Every night, they met by the mango trees to tell each other stories. Together, they would laugh and laugh and laugh . . .

PHILLY *continues to weave her story.*

The end.

ACKNOWLEDGEMENTS

We wrote most of this play in Toronto (Tkaronto) and we'd like to acknowledge the privilege of creating on this land that has been cared for by the Wendat, the Haudenosaunee, and the Anishinabek First Nations, including the Mississaugas of the Credit. As settlers, we honour the original caretakers of this land and acknowledge our shared responsibility in caring for it.

To Nina Lee Aquino, you are embedded into every landscape in Uwi. Thank you for being our dramaturge, our director, and one of our biggest champions. To Paula Wing, thank you for uplifting us and the play with your curiosity, wonder, and childlike joy. To MB, thank you for being there and believing in this story from the beginning. To our original cast and creative team, thank you for bringing Uwi and its characters to life. To all the actors and artists that helped us develop our play through workshops and readings throughout the years, thank you for your artistry and for journeying with us as we shaped the story. Thank you to the people from the theatre companies and organizations that believed in and supported our work, including Leon Aureus, Pat Bradley, Marjorie Chan, Ins Choi, Courtney Ch'ng Lancaster, Stephen Colella, Lucy Eveleigh, Pablo Felices-Luna, Rong Fu, Lynda Hill, Andrea Kwan, Laura Paduch, Alan Quismorio, Renna Reddie, Miquelon Rodriguez, Leah-Simone Bowen, John Van Burek, Guillermo Verdecchia, and David Yee. Thanks to Haniely Pableo for helping us with the Tagalog incantations. Thank you to the Playwrights Canada Press team—Annie, Blake, and Jessica—for guiding us through our first publishing experience.

To the young ones in our family, thank you for inspiring us to write this story. We hope you see yourselves in it. And to the rest of our Abalos, Halili, Maceda, and Mapili families, thank you for your unending love and support.

Finally, we honour each other as co-creators and partners. We're thankful for our connection and this shared journey.

Andrea Mapili and Byron Abalos are Filipinx-Canadian multidisciplinary artists. Andrea is a playwright, movement director, choreographer, dancer, and somatic practitioner. Byron is a playwright, actor, and producer, working in theatre, film, and television. In 2017, they produced the Toronto premiere of *Cassettes 100* by Andrea's grandfather, José Maceda, at the Young Centre for the Performing Arts. *Through the Bamboo* is their first co-written play and their first play for young audiences. They currently live in Tkaronto with their daughter, Mayari, who was named after the Philippine goddess of the moon, revolution, and equality, and was born shortly after the premiere of *Through the Bamboo*.

First edition: June 2021
Printed and bound in Canada by Rapido Books, Montreal

Jacket design by Marshall Lorenzo
Author photo © Jenna Harris

**PLAYWRIGHTS
CANADA PRESS**
202-269 Richmond St. W.
Toronto, ON
M5V 1X1

416.703.0013
info@playwrightscanada.com
www.playwrightscanada.com
@playcanpress